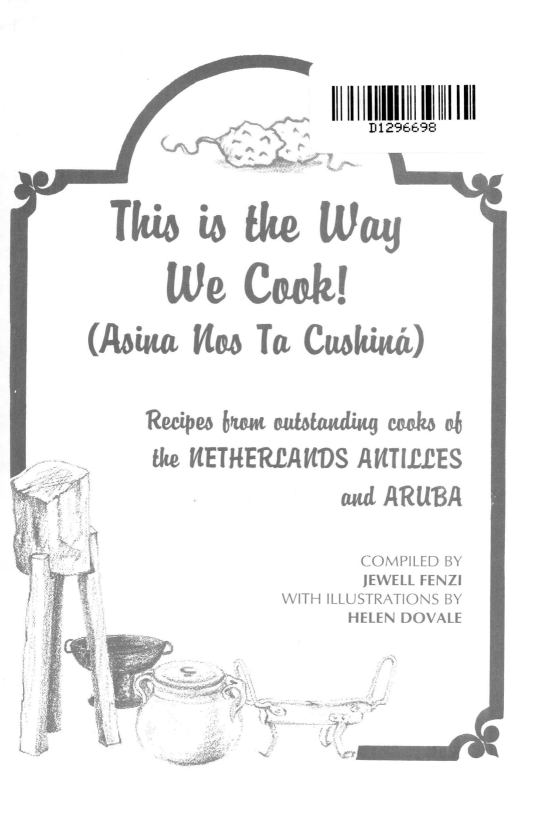

This is the Way We Cook!
(Asina Nos Ta Cushiná)

Recipes from outstanding cooks of
the NETHERLANDS ANTILLES
and ARUBA

COMPILED BY
JEWELL FENZI
WITH ILLUSTRATIONS BY
HELEN DOVALE

THE NETHERLANDS ANTILLES

are a collection of six islands geographically divided into two groups and widely separated by the Caribbean Sea. Aruba, Curaçao, and Bonaire comprise the southern cluster, or Leeward Island, which are located just north of the Venezuelan coast. A trio of smaller islands, Sint Maarten, Saba, and Sint Eustatius, forms the northern or Windward group. They are near Puerto Rico, and lie some 500 miles northeast of the Leeward Islands. English is most commonly spoken in the Windward group, but the southern islanders are usually tri- or quadri-lingual. They speak Dutch, English, and Spanish, as well as Papiamento, the local lilting tongue which envolved from numerous European languages and African dialects.

Like Papiamento, the cuisine of the Leeward Islands represents a mingling of diverse cultures. The zest and tang of Southern dishes came with the Sephardic Jews from Spain, Portugal, and Latin America. The Dutch brought the exotica of Indonesia, as well as their own hearty, robust cooking. The piquancy of West Africa is also there. In general, the recipes with Papiamento titles are exclusive to these islands. The Windward dishes are listed in English and many reflect the Leeward cultural influences; however, their black-eyed peas, peanuts, sweet potatoes, and pigs' tails bring to mind traditional cooking in the southern United States.

With this mingled heritage, but with limited ingredients for imports were sporadic and most of the islands produced little, early Antillean cooks developed their distinctive cuisine. A treasure chest of their recipes, handed down from generation, may be sampled for the first time in these pages. *Bon Probecho!**

*Papiamento for Bon Appétit

Note:
When "This is the Way We Cook" was written in 1971, Aruba was part of the Netherlands Antilles. On January 1, 1986, the island became an autonomous member of the Kingdom of the Netherlands. The cuisine, however, retains its distinctive Antillean flavor, and the recipes in this little volume remain authentic.

First printing 1971 - Eleventh printing 2003
ISBN 99904-943-7-1

Printed in Aruba by ProGraphics Inc.
Distributed by DeWit & VanDorp Stores
L.G. Smith Boulevard 110
P.O. Box 386 - Oranjestad - Aruba

Table of
CONTENTS

At the marketplace

Appetizers

Empaná (Filled Corn-Meal Crescents) *3 Dozen*

For the corn-meal crust, bring to a boil in the top of a double boiler but directly over the flame:

4 ½ cups water
1 tsp. salt

Slowly add:

4 cups yellow corn-meal
blended with 4 cups cold water

Cook for a few minutes, stirring constantly. Place over boiling water and cook an additional ten minutes. Mixture will be very thick.
Remove from fire and add:

1 cup sharp cheese, grated
2 green plantains, boiled and mashed

When mixture is cool enough to handle, knead well to blend the dough. Add:

Up to 1 cup flour

to make dough more pliable.
For the filling, sauté in three tablespoons butter:

1 lb. ground round steak

When the meat is browned, add and simmer until reduced and almost dry:

2 medium tomatoes, peeled and chopped
2 medium onions, minced
1 small green pepper, minced
1 piece hot pepper minced
or ½ tsp. Tabasco sauce

Add and mix well:

1 Tbs. capers
¼ cup green olives, chopped
¼ cup raisins, chopped
¼ tsp. nutmeg
Salt and pepper

Spread three tablespoons of the corn-meal in a circle on a damp cloth. Place one tablespoon filling on one half of the circle. Fold into a crescent and seal the edges with a fork. Fry in deep, hot fat until golden brown. *Empanás* may be prepared in advance and warmed in the oven just before serving.

4

Pastechis   (Spicy, Filled Pastries)   *4 Dozen*

The versatile *pastechi* is a plump little pastry filled with spicy meat, shrimp or fish. It appears everywhere and around the clock - at coffee, tea or cocktails, at beach parties or on the most formal buffet tables. Surprisingly light and delicous, *pastechis* should be prepared in abundance for they disappear rapidly. *Pastechis* are called *patties* in the Windward Islands.

Prepare the meat filling for *keshi yená*, page 28
Sift and set aside:

> *6 cups flour*

Cream:

> *3 heaping Tbs. butter*
> *3 heaping Tbs. shortening*
> *1½ Tbs. salt*
> *1 or 2 eggs*

Add two cups of the sifted flour to the shortening mixture.
Add, a little at a time:

> *1½ cups water*

Continue adding flour two cups at a time until it is absorbed in the mixture. When the dough is pliable, knead it well. Roll the dough into a very thin sheet, then cut out circles about three inches in diameter.
Place one tablespoon filling in the center of one pastry circle. Top it with a second circle. Lightly moisten edges and press the circles together. Fold or roll the edges over slightly and flute them as pie crust. Fry the *pastechis* in deep, hot fat until golden brown. They may be prepared in advance and heated in the oven just before serving.

Bolita di Keshi   (Cheese Balls)   *3 Dozen*

Grate finely and toss together:

> *1 lb. sharp yellow cheese*
> *(cheddar or oude boerenkaas)*
> *1 lb. keshi di buriko*
> *(or any white cheese such as fromage blanc,*
> *queso blanco, ricotto, feta, etc.)*

Stir in:

> *6 eggs, beaten*
> *5 Tbs. cornstarch*

Shape the mixture into small balls. These may be kept indefinitely in the freezer. Drop the balls into deep, hot fat and fry until golden. Serve piping hot on toothpicks

Cala   (Black-Eyed Pea Puffs)   *2 Dozen*

A spicy, different cocktail snack, this tidbit has been called "an edible souvenir of the Antilles".

Soak overnight in ample water:

> $^1/_2$ *lb. boonchi wowo pretu, or black-eyed peas*
> *1 tsp. salt*

Place the peas in the folds of a towel and rub vigorously to remove skins. Discard the skin and dry the peas thoroughly. Put them through a food grinder.

Beat in:

> $^1/_4$ *tsp. cayenne*
> *1 tsp. salt*

While beating, add a little at a time:

> $^1/_2$ *cup water*

Continue beating until batter is fluffy and double the original quantity. Drop by teaspoonfuls into deep, hot fat. Remove when golden brown and drain on absorbent paper. Serve piping hot.

Tequeños   (Cheese Sticks in Pastry)   *2 Dozen*

Divide in half the ingredients of the pastry recipe for *pastechis*. Roll the dough into a thin sheet. Cut it into strips, one inch wide and seven or eight inches long.
Cut into rectangels one and one-half inches long and about one-quarter inch thick.

> *1$^1/_2$ lbs. sharp yellow cheese*

Wrap pastry around the cheese sticks, bandage style, and seal the ends. Fry the *tequeños* in deep, hot fat until golden brown. Serve piping hot.

Banana Chips   *3 Dozen*

In the Antilles the plantain, which is inedible until cooked, is called *banana*. The *banana* usually associated with corn flakes is called *bacoba*. To avoid confusion, *bananas* are referred to as *plantains* in these recipes.
Select a very green plantain, the greener the better. Slice it thinly into rounds. Drop the rounds one by one into hot fat. They will become golden almost immediately. Remove rounds to absorbent paper and sprinkle with salt. As soon as they are cool, store them in a tightly closed tin. Chips can be made a few days in advance, but will become limp if left exposed to humid and tropical air.

Omelette

Here are two versions of the outer, or omelette, part of the recipe. The one without flour is perhaps more delicate. Both make enough batter for six very thin pancakes about ten inches in diameter.

PANCAKE I

Beat:

>1 egg

Add:

>1 Tbs. milk
>Salt and pepper to taste

Lightly grease a frying pan with butter, removing any excess with absorbent paper. Add the egg and tilt the pan to distribute the batter evenly. Cook the egg slowly, but thoroughly, over a low flame. The pancake should be very thin. Repeat this process six times.

PANCAKE II

Sift:

>$^1/_2$ cup self rising flour
>Pinch of salt

Add:

>1 egg, well beaten
>$^1/_2$ cup milk

Follow cooking directions for Pancake I.

FILLING

Sauté lightly in two tablespoons butter:

>1 small onion, minced
>$^1/_2$ hot pepper, minced, or $^1/_2$ tsp. Tabasco sauce

Add:

>1 Tbs. parsley, chopped
>$^1/_2$ tsp. lime juice
>1 Tbs. ketchup
>1 seven-ounce tin shrimp or tuna, finely minced

Place the pancake on a flat surface and sparsely spread a bit of the filling in a narrow line, from edge to edge, across the center. Omelettes should not be too thick, so be sparing with the filling. Fold the pancake in half and roll it as illustrated. Chill the omelette thoroughly, then cut it into sections about one and one-half inches long. Skewer with a toothpick.

Grate

>About $^1/_2$ cup Parmesan Cheese

over omelettes on a serving plate. Omelettes are sometimes decorated with a drop of ketchup where the toothpick is to be inserted.

Zult   (Pickled Pigs' Ears)

Serves 12

Not a silk purse this, but a delectable local dish which must be tried to be appreciated.

Scrub thoroughly until they are white:

> *1 lb. pigs' ears*

Place them in an enamel or pyrex saucepan with salted water to cover. Bring to a brisk boil and cook the ears for twenty minutes or until tender. Drain the ears, reserving one-half cup of the liquid, and slice into julienne strips.
Make a marinade of:

> *2 cups white vinager*
> *2 to 3 cloves garlic, crushed*
> *1 tsp allspice*
> *12 clavos, or cloves*
> *2 onions, sliced*
> *2 or more hot peppers in small pieces*
> *The one-half cup reserved broth*

No salt is necessary. Cover the pigs' ears with the marinade and refrigerate for twenty-four hours. Zult is *pika* or spicy hot, and happily accompanied by little chunks of French bread.

Antillean Antipasto

About 4 Cups

Drain, then toss together:

> *1 tin sardines*
> *1 tin tuna*

Add:

> *Juice of one lime*

Break the fish into chunks, but not flakes. Set aside.
Mix well:

> *1 four-ounce tin pimentos, chopped*
> *1½ cups chopped, mixed pickles*
> *(include sweet, sour and dill pick, and cocktail onions)*
> *1 cup pimento olives, sliced*
> *1 twelve-ounce bottle ketchup*
> *1 Tbs. Lea and Perrins sauce*
> *Few drops Tabasco sauce*
> *(½ cup sliced mushrooms)*

Add fish and chill well. Serve with crackers as an hors d'oeuvre, or in a lettuce cup as an appetizer. The antipasto may be made in advance and frozen. Add additional seasonings if necessary after defrosting.

Bitterbal (Meat Croquettes)

2 Dozen

The "bitter" refers to the accompanying drink, not the appetizer. These are mild, crustly little balls to be dipped in tangy mustard.

Make a thick white sauce of

> 3 Tbs. butter
> 3 Tbs. flour
> $^3/_4$ cup stock

Add:

> 1$^1/_2$ cups finely chopped, cooked meat (roast beef or veal, ham, chicken or shrimp)
> 1 Tbs. parsley, minced
> $^1/_2$ tsp. Worcestershire sauce
> Salt and pepper to taste

Chill mixture and shape into balls one inch in diameter. Roll balls in:

> Fine cracker crumbs

Then dip them in a mixture of:

> 1 egg, beaten
> 2 Tbs. water

Dip again in cracker crumbs. Fry the balls in deep, hot fat for one or two minutes, or until golden brown. Serve hot with mustard. Spear with toothpicks.

Carcó (Pickled Conch)

Serve 12

Bonaire fisherman search for *carcó,* or conch, "two arms's lengths down" in the shallow water of Lac Baai. Their conch catch is considered an island delicacy, whether pickled, stewed, or curried, or dropped into the kettle to lend a savory taste to *sòpi di carcó,* page 18.

Clean and peel:

> 1 lb. carcó, or conch

Pound the conch well with a wooden mallet. In a heavy saucepan, bring several cups of salted water to a brisk boil. Drop the conch into the boiling water and cook only a few minutes. The conch becomes tough and loses its succelence if overcooked. Drain well and cut the conch into bite-size pieces. Make the marinade for *zult,* page 8. Cover the conch with the marinade and refrigerate for twenty-four hours. Serve with saltines.

Sòpi di Banana   (Green Plantain Soup)   *Serves 4 - 6*

Harking back to the pre-frozen food days, many Antillean recipes call for salted meats. Traditionalists insist upon its flavor, but fresh meats may be substituted if the salt content is adjusted.

Soak overnight in ample water:

> *1 lb. salted beef*

Discard water, and place the beef in a heavy kettle with:

> *4 cups fresh water*
> *1 clove garlic*
>   *Few sprigs parsley*
> *1 or 2 celery stalks, with leaves*
> *2 scallions*
> *1 bay leaf, slightly crushed*
> *1 tsp. salt*

Bring to a brisk boil. Reduce heat and simmer until meat is tender. Strain broth, discarding the vegetables. Dice the beef and set aside.
Return the broth to the fire and bring again to a gentle boil.
Add:

> *2 tsp. Worcestershire sauce*
> *1 Tbs. tomato sauce*
> *$^{1}/_{2}$ cup chopped celery*

Slice into thick rounds:

> *2 very green plantians*

Fry until golden in two or three tablespoon butter. Pound each round with a wooden mallet until flat, and add immediately to the soup. Simmer an additional fifteen minutes. During the last few minutes cooking time add:

> *$1^{1}/_{2}$ cups shredded cabbage*
>   *The diced beef*
> *1 cinnamon stick*

Discard cinnamon stick before serving the soup.

Avocado Soup

Place in the container of an electric blender:

1 large avocado, peeled, seeded and cubed
1 1/2 cups chicken broth, strained
to remove fat globules
1 clove garlic, crushed
Generous dash Tabasco sauce

Cover and blend on high speed until ingredients are thoroughly puréed.

Remove cover and add:

1 1/2 cups cream

Cover and blend a few additional seconds. If the mixture is too thick, thin with a little cream or broth. Correct seasonings, adding more Tabasco sauce and a pinch of salt to taste. Serve well chilled. Garnish with chopped chives or parsley.

Peanut Soup

Serves 6

A local dish frequently found on the menu at Capitain's Quarters, the charming Windwardside hotel located in the old residence of one of Saba's famed sea capitains. The peanuts were formerly ground by mortar and pestle, but peanut butter makes the soup infinitely easier to prepare!

Place in the top of a double boiler:

1/2 cup peanut butter

Add gradually, stirring until well blended:

1 cup chicken broth, rich and simmering

Stir in:

1/2 small onion, very finely grated
Salt of taste
Generous dash of Tabasco sauce

Cook these ingredients in the double boiler for about fifteen minutes. Stir in:

1 cup milk
1 cup chicken broth

Simmer the soup an additional few minutes until it is creamy. If the soup is too thick, add more milk and adjust seasonings. If it is too thin, blend in more peanut butter, a tablespoonful at a time. Peanut Soup in an excellent first course, but is rich and only small servings are necesarry.

Callalu Soup

Thyme lends a savory touch to this thick soup. If spinach is substituted for callalu, a little lime juice should be added for tartness.

Soak over night in ample water:

   2 salted pigs' tails

Drain the tails well and place them in a heavy kettle with six cups of fresh water. Bring them to a rapid boil. Reduce heat and simmer for forty minutes or until the tails are tender. Leaving the kettle on the flame, remove the tails from the broth. When they are cool enough to handle, cut them into serving pieces and return them to the kettle.
Wash and chop:

   2 medium bunches callalu
   (or use 3 ten-ounce packages frozen chopped spinach)

Add callalu and the following ingredients to the broth:

   4 or 5 sweet potatoes, peeled and diced
   1 medium onion, sliced
   1 clove garlic, minced
   1 sprig fresh thyme
   1 Tbs. butter
   Pinch of black pepper

Simmer the soup for about one half hour. If it becomes too thick, add a little boiling water.

Sopito   (Fish and Coconut Soup)   *Serves 6*

From Aruba to Sint Maarten, good Antillean cooks always have a kettle of boiling water on the back of the stove. Here it is used to coax along the zesty creole sauce.

Soak overnight:

>$^1/_2$ *lb. salted beef*
>$^1/_2$ *lb. salted cod*

Salt and pepper a:

>*1$^1/_2$ lb. red snapper*

Then rub it with a mixture of:

>$^1/_4$ *tsp. nutmeg*   *1 tsp. Tabasco sauce*
>*1 clove garlic*
>*1 or 2 Tbs. lime juice*

Set the red snapper aside for an hour. Discard the water from the beef and cod and place beef in a heavy kettle with:

>*4 cups fresh water*   *1 or 2 celery stalks*
>*2 carrots*   *1 leek*
>*2 onions*   *1 sprig of mint*

Bring to brisk boil. Reduce heat and simmer until beef is tender, about an hour. Add the cod and simmer for several minutes until the fish flakes when tested with the tines of a fork. Remove the beef and cod from the broth. Cube the meat, debone and flake fish. Set aside. Strain broth, discarding the vegetables, and return it to the fire.

Sauté in two or three tablespoons butter until the onion is transparent:

>*1 onion, minced*
>*1 small green pepper, chopped*

Add:

>*1 large tomato, peeled and chopped*
>*2 Tbs. tomato paste*

Simmer a few minutes, then add the seasoned snapper. Cover the fish with boiling water and simmer until it flakes when tested with a fork. Remove snapper form the sauce. Debone, leaving the fish in bite-size chunks, and set aside. Reduce the sauce to a rich paste, adding a bit of boiling water from time to time to prolong cooking. Strain sauce into the simmering beef stock.

Add to taste:

>*Tabasco sauce*
>*Salt and pepper*

Blend in:

>*1 or 2 Tbs. corn-meal mixed with $^1/_4$ cup cold water*

During the last few minutes cooking time add, but do not permit to boil:

>*1 cup coconut milk, page 43*
>*The cod, snapper and beef*

Serve with *funchi*.

13

Sòpi di Pampuna   (Pumpkin Soup)   *Serves 6*

Ruku, the seed of the annatto tree found in the Caribbean, is used to enhance the appearance of this delicate soup. Heat several *ruku* in a cup of hot oil. Let stand until the oil absorbs the deep orange color of the seeds. Discard the *ruku* and add several teaspoons of the oil to the soup.

Soak overnight in water to cover:

   $^1/_4$ lb. salted beef

Discard water, and place the beef in a heavy kettle with:

4 cups fresh water	*$^1/_4$ tsp. thyme*
1 or 2 celery stalks	*1 large onion*
1 or 2 leeks	*$^1/_2$ tsp. Tabasco sauce*

Bring to a brisk boil. Reduce heat and simmer for an hour until meat is tender. Strain the broth, discarding vegetables. Dice the beef and set aside. Return the broth to the fire and simmer until tender:

   2 lbs. pumpkin, peeled and cubed
   2 large potatoes, peeled and cubed

During the last few minutes of cooking time add:

   1 cinnamon stick
   1 Tbs. sugar

Remove from heat and discard cinnamon stick. Place the pumpkin, potatoes and the broth in the container of an electric blender and purée. Slowly add:

   1 cup cream
   2 Tbs. butter

Heat the soup gently, but do not boil. Just before serving, add the diced beef and the *ruku* coloring.

Cadushi   (Cactus Soup)   *Serves 6*

Traditional *cadushi,* or cactus soup recipes, begin with, "Buy a few cents worth of cactus powder in the market". Continue with the directions for *giambo,* page 17, following the instructions until the red snapper has been prepared. Then instead of okra, add the cactus powder. Return the cubed beef and red snapper pieces to the kettle, heat thoroughly and adjust seasonings. *Cadushi* also has a slippery consistency, and is a favorite of islanders living in the *kunuku,* or countryside.

Sòpi di Yuwana   (Iguana Soup)   *Serves 6 - 8*

Small boys in the *kunuku* snare *yuwana,* or iguana, and offer them for sale along the roadsides. Choose a plump one for this delicacy, which reputedly tastes either like rabbit or chicken.

Clean, skin and cut into serving pieces:

> *1 iguana*

Place in a heavy kettle:

> *1$\frac{1}{2}$ quarts water and 2 chicken bouillon cubes*
> *or broth form the keshi yená recipe, page 28*
> *1 clove garlic*
> *1 leek*
> *1 tomato, coarsley chopped*
> *1 onion, studded with 3 cloves*
> *1 green pepper, quartered*
> *$\frac{1}{4}$ of a small cabbage*

Bring to a boil, reduce heat and simmer for thirty minutes. Add the iguana, and simmer an additional half hour, or until the meat is tender. Remove from the fire. Strain broth, discarding vegetables. Bone the iguana and set the meat aside.

Return the broth to the fire and add:

> *1 tsp. cumin, or to taste*
> *Dash of nutmeg*
> *Salt and pepper*
> *A few ounces of vermicelli*

Simmer for about five minutes until the vermicelli is tender. Add the iguana and heat thoroughly. Serve piping hot with *funchi*.

Pía ku Mondongo   (Tripe Soup)   *Serve 6 - 8*

Fresh fruits and vegetables are brought to the islands by sailing schooners from Venezuela, the Dominican Republic, and Grenada. The many ingredients for *pía ku mondongo* are easily found at these picturesque "floating markets".

Wash well and rub with lime juice:

> *1 lb. tripe*
> *2 calves feet*

Place meat in a heavy kettle with:

> *2 quarts water*
> *2 small onions*
> *1 or 2 cloves garlic, sliced*
> *2 stalks celery with leaves*
> *2 medium green peppers*
> *2 large tomatoes*
> *1 or 2 leeks*
> *1 tsp. salt*
> *At least one hot pepper*

Bring to a brisk boil. Reduce heat and simmer for two hours, or until meat is tender. Remove from heat and permit the meat to cool in the broth. Cut tripe in small pieces; remove meat from the calve's feet, discarding bones. Strain broth and discard vegetables. This may be done a day in advance, in which case the meat and broth should be refrigerated.

Return the broth to the fire and add, simmering until tender:

> *2 carrots, cut into strips*
> *$1/2$ small pumpkin, peeled and cubed*
> *1 or 2 beef bouillon cubes*

Ten minutes later add:

> *1 firm plantain, cut into rounds*
> *2 sweet potatoes, peeled and cubed*

Fifteen minutes later add:

> *3 potatoes, peeled and cubed*
> *$1/4$ cup raisins*

Ten minutes later add:

> *The tripe and clave's feet*
> *3 corn-on-the-cob, broken in half*
> *1 tsp. capers*
> *1 Tsp. Lime juice*

Simmer five minutes. Adjust seasonings and serve. If desired, add during the last few minutes cooking time:

> *$1/2$ cabbage, shredded*
> *1 pkg. frozen green beans*

Giambo   (Okra Soup)   *Serve 6 - 8*

Giambo (pronounced ghee-Yam-bo) is the Antillean gumbo, a thick, hearty soup. The puréed okra gives it a slippery consistency.

Soak overnight:

> ½ lb. salted beef

Discard water. Place the beef in a heavy kettle with:

> 2 quarts fresh water
> 1 ham hock
> 1 or 2 onions
>   A few sprigs of parsley
> 1 or 2 carrots
> 1 bay leaf
> 1 celery stalk

Bring to a brisk boil. Reduce heat and simmer for about one and a half hours, or until meat is tender.
Place in the simmering kettle.

> 1 lb. red snapper fillets

After a few minutes test the fish with the tines of a fork, and remove from the broth when it flakes easily. Make bite-size chunks of the fillets. Remove the beef from the broth, cube and set aside with the fish. Strain the broth and return it to the fire. Discard the ham hock and vegetables.
To the simmering broth add:

> 2 lbs. okra, washed and sliced
>   A few sprigs crushed yerba di hole, or fresh basil
> ½ tsp. black pepper

Simmer until the okra is tender. With a *lele stick,* or its equivalent, a wire whisk, reduce the okra to a purée. Return the cubed beef and red snapper pieces to the kettle. Heat thoroughly and adjust seasonings.
Garnish *giambo* with:

> ¼ lb. cooked shrimp

Funchi is a "must" with this delicous soup.

A lele stick against the soup pot.

Sòpi di Carcò   (Conch Soup)   *Serves 4*

Wash and trim:

> *1 lb. conch*

**Dry the conch thoroughly, then pound it with a floured wooden mallet.
Rub the conch with.**

> *2 Tbs. lime juice*

**Cut it into bite-size pieces and set aside for later use.
In heavy kettle bring to a brisk boil:**

> *1½ quarts rich chicken broth*   *1 green pepper, sliced*
> *1 tomato, peeled*   *1 clove garlic, slivered*
> *1 onion sliced*   *A sprig of fresh basil*

**Reduce heat and simmer for about twenty minutes. Remove broth from fire
and strain, discarding vegetables. Return broth to the fire and add:**

> *1 cup carrots, diced*

**Simmer for about twenty minutes.
Add:**

> *The conch*
> *Salt and pepper*
> *½ package vermicelli (about 4 ounces)*
> *4 or 6 drops Tabasco sauce*

**Simmer an additional ten minutes, or just until the conch is tender.
Do not overcook or the conch will lose its succulence.**

Sòpi di Binja   (Wine Soup)   *Serves 10 - 12*

E sopi aki ta lamta morto. **This soup is strong enough to wake the dead!
An Antillean favorite, wine soup is mentioned in the writings of Petronius
as early as 57 A.D.
In a large saucepan, bring six cups of water to a rapid boil and add:**

> *30 prunes*   *1 or 2 cinnamon sticks*

**Reduce the heat, and simmer the prunes until they are soft. Remove the
saucepan from the fire and permit it to cool. Discard the cinnamon sticks,
and remove the prunes from the liquid, setting them aside for later use.
Stir into the cooled liquid:**

> *½ cup cornstarch, mixed with enough water to make
> a smooth paste*

**Return the saucepan to a low flame, and stir the liquid until it thickens.
Add and bring to a boil:**

> *2 one-fifth bottles dry red wine*
> *¾ cup sugar*

**Stir until the sugar is dissolved. The soup should have body and a smooth
consistency. If it is too thick, add water a little at a time. Add the prunes
just before serving.**

Erwten Soep   (Pea Soup)

Serves 6 - 8

Two things which The Netherlands acquired as a result of the Eighty Year War, 1568 - 1648, were her independence and this robust pea soup from Spain, which was exported soon afterward to the Antilles.

Wash thoroughly, then soak overnight:

> *2 cups split peas*

Drain peas, reserving the liquid.
Place in a heavy kettle:

> *The reserved liquid, plus enough water to make 3 quarts*

Add:

> *A ham hock or cube of salt pork*
> *2 onions*   *2 carrots*
> *1 celery stalk with leaves*
> *1 clove garlic*   *1 bay leaf*
> *1/4 tsp. Rosemary*
> *(Piece of hot pepper)*

Bring to a brisk boil, reduce heat and simmer for about forty five minutes. Strain broth, discarding vegetables. Skim off any accumulation of grease; or chill the strained broth, and easily remove congealed grease. Return broth to the fire with the meat and add the soaked peas. Simmer for three hours, or until peas are tender. Strain, return the liquid to the fire. Purée the peas in a food mill and return them to the broth.
As a thickening add:

> *2 Tbs. butter*
> *2 Tbs. flour*

to a little cooled soup mixture. Blend well and stir it into the kettle.
Add a heat thoroughly:

> *1/2 lb. sliced, smoked sausage*

Stir the soup well before ladling it into a serving tureen.
Serve with *funchi*.

19

Fish

Scabechi   (Pickled Fish - Cooked)   *Serves 12*

One Aruba cook, reminiscing about her childhood, recalls that *scabechi* was always on hand in the family larder. It kept well, even before the days of refrigeration, and was brought out to treat unexpected guests.

Fry in two or three tablespoons butter until golden:

> *2 lb. mackerel, kingfish or any white fish*

Place the fish in a deep earthenware bowl.
For the marinade, sauté lightly in two tablespoons oil:

> *6 small onions, sliced*

Add and bring to a boil:

> *1$\frac{1}{2}$ cups water*
> *$\frac{1}{2}$ cup white wine vinegar*
> *4 small carrots, sliced very thinly lengthwise*
> *4 hot peppers, cut in eights*
> *3 bay leaves*
> *2 tsp. salt*
> *12 peppercorns*

The following may be added to make a more flavorful marinade:

> *2 cloves garlic, crushed*
> *1 Tbs. capers*
> *6 or 8 pimento olives, sliced*

Pour the marinade over the fish and let stand for at least twenty-four hours. *Scabechi* may be served either as a cold appetizer or as a hot fish course. It should be reheated gently just before serving.

20

Lobster Vinaigrette

Serves 20

Mix well:

      $1\frac{1}{2}$ cups oil
      2 cups white wine vinegar
      1 Tbs. piccalilly, or mustard pickle
      1 tsp. sugar
      1 tsp. salt

Mince and add:

      4 large onions
      2 hot peppers
      1 clove garlic
      $\frac{1}{3}$ cup capers, or to taste

Plunge into rapidly boiling water:

      5 lbs. lobster or shrimp

Simmer for twenty minutes. Shell and clean.

Marinate the shellfish in the sauce for several days before serving.

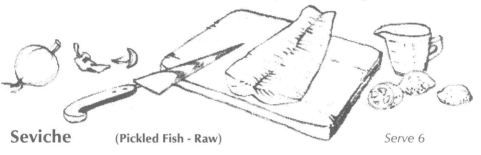

Seviche   **(Pickled Fish - Raw)**

Serve 6

Halibut is recommended, and small-boned fish should be avoided, in this recipe. *Seviche* makes an excellent toothpick tidbit, or may be served on shredded lettuce as an appetizer. Small servings are sufficient as it very *pika*.

Cut into bite-size pieces:

      1 lb. any white fish

Make a marinade of:

      $1\frac{1}{2}$ cups lemon juice, or enough to cover fish
      $1\frac{1}{2}$ cups onion, finely chopped
      1 or 2 cloves garlic, sliced
      $\frac{1}{2}$ hot pepper, cut into 3 pieces
      (or 1 tsp. Tabasco sauce)
      1 or 2 tsp. salt

Pour the sauce over the fish and marinate for at least twenty-four hours. The fish will lose its translucence and become opaque, as if cooked.

Salmau na Pekel   (Pickled Salmon)   *Serves 10*

Two festive occasions at Club Curaçao are December 26, Second Christmas Day, and Queen Juliana's birthday celebration on April 30. *Salmau na pekel* is always found on the sumptuous buffet tables prepared for these events.

Soak in abundant water for a day:

>2 ½ lbs. salted salmon

Change water several times to speed removal of the salt. Clean the salmon, debone and cut into strips.
Thinly slice:

>3 medium onions

Soften the onions by permitting them to stand for a while in hot water. Drain the onions well.
Combine:

>1 cup white wine vinegar
>3 Tbs. olive oil

Add and blend well:

>1 hot pepper, minced
>3 cloves garlic, crushed
>2 bay leaves, slightly bruised
>10 cloves
>1 Tbs. capers
>Pimento olives to taste

In a serving bowl alternate layers of the salmon, the onions and the marinade.
Let stand for twenty-four hours.

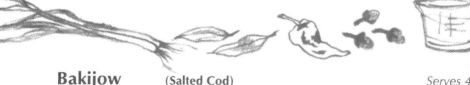

Bakijow   (Salted Cod)   *Serves 4*

The piquancy of this cod dish is tempered by the bland avocado.

Soak overnight in ample water:

>1 salted cod, or bakijow

Flake, debone and marinate twenty-four hours in:

>1 cup French dressing
>½ cup onions, minced
>1 tsp. Tabasco sauce

To serve, heap the marinated cod in the hollows of two halved avocados.

Stuffed Crab Backs

Serves 6

Blue crabs inhabiting the crater of Sint Eustatia's volcanic Quill emerge at night to forage. The enterprising Statians hike up to the crater to hunt the crabs by flashlight, and their catch is frequently used to create this island delicacy.

Drop into ample boiling salted water and simmer for twenty minutes:

> *16 to 20 blue crabs*

Drain the crabs well, and when they are cool enough to handle removes as much of the meat as possible. Scrub the back shells thoroughly; dry them and butter each one lightly. Set the shells aside for later use. Grind the crab meat in a food mill with the following ingredients:

> *1 medium oninon, minced*
> *3 sprigs of chives, chopped*
> *1 small green pepper, chopped*
> *6 slices dry bread, soaked in milk and then squeezed*

Lightly sauté the ground mixture in one-fourth cup butter, adding the following ingredients:

> *2 Tbs. Worcestershire sauce*
> *A pinch of chopped, fresh thyme*
> *1 or 2 Tbs. tomato paste*
> *Salt and pepper*

Fill the crab backs with the meat mixture, then dust them with:

> *Bread crumbs*

Dot each shell with butter and place under the broiler for a few minutes until filling is bubbly and golden.

Stewed Lobster & Dumplings *Serves 4*

This superb dish can best be made in a wide earthenware casserole which can be tightly covered and used directly over the flame.

Drop into a kettle of rapidly boiling water:

1 live lobster

Simmer it briefly, or only until the lobster turns red. Do not overcook, for the lobster pieces simmer later in the sauce.
Remove the meat from the shell and cut it into bite size pieces.

Sauté in one or two tablespoons butter:

1 large onion, sliced

When the onion is transparent add:

2 tomatoes peeled and chopped
1 Tbs. ketchup
Dash of black pepper
Dash of thyme

Simmer these ingredients for twenty minutes then add the lobster pieces and:

3 cups boiling water

Stir in:

1 Tbs. white wine vinegar   *2 or 3 beef bouillon cubes*
Salt to taste   *1 tsp. Worcestershire sauce*

While lobster simmers for about fifteen minutes over a very low flame, combine the following ingredient for the dumpling:

2 cups sifted flour
1 tsp. baking powder
1 tsp. salt

Stir in water, a few tablespoonfuls at a time, until the mixture has the consistency of a very thick batter. Drop the dumplings by spoonfuls into the simmering lobster. Cover the casserole tightly and let the dumplings cook for a few minutes. Turn them gently over once with a fork. If the sauce has cooked away too rapidly, add a bit of boiling water and let the casserole simmer for another few minutes until the dumplings have finished cooking.
Serve the dish immediately with fried plantains.

Red Snapper Curaçao Style

Perhaps the most widely known island dish, Red Snapper Curaçao Style is usually served with *funchi* and fried plantains. One cook insists the menu be varied by replacing *funchi* with carrot rice.

Prepare for frying:

>   *2 lbs. fillet of red snapper*

Make a marinade of:

>   *$\frac{1}{2}$ cup lime juice*
>   *2 or 3 scallions, finely chopped*
>   *1 clove garlic, minced*
>   *Salt and pepper to taste*

Rub the fish with the marinade and set it aside for at least an hour.

Melt in a heavy skillet.

>   *3 or 4 Tbs. butter*

Cut the fillets in serving pieces and coat them with:

>   *Flour*

When the skillet is very hot, fry the fish quickly until it is nicely browned and crisp. Place in a baking dish and keep it warm in the oven.
In the fish drippings sauté until the onion is transparent:

>   *1 large onion, chopped*
>   *1 medium green pepper, chopped*
>   *2 cloves garlic, crushed*

Add and simmer about twenty minutes:

>   *2 large tomatoes, or 6 plum tomatoes,*
>   *peeled and chopped*
>   *Salt and pepper to taste*

The creole sauce should be rich and thick. Just before serving place the red snapper pieces in the sauce and heat them thoroughly.
To make carrot rice, sauté lightly in butter one minced onion and a grated carrot. Stir them into simmering rice when the water is almost absorbed.

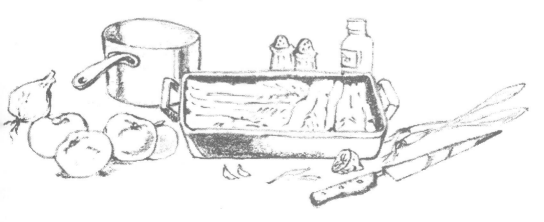

Balchi di Pisca   (Fish Balls)   *Serve 6*

These delectable fish balls can also be made with salmon or fish fillets. Substitute one large can of salmon or one pound of any white fish for the cod.

Soak for twenty-four hours:

> *1 salted cod, or bakijow*

Discard the water. Place cod in saucepan with fresh water to cover. Simmer gently until the fish flakes easily when tested with the tines of a fork. Strain, reserving a bit of the broth.
Debone the cod and set it aside for later use.
In a saucepan, bring to boil in water to cover:

> *3 medium potatoes, peeled and diced*

When the potatoes are tender, drain them well. Add the cod and mash the two ingredients thoroughly together.

Place in the container of an electric blender:

> *1 tomato, peeled and chopped*
> *1/2 green pepper, chopped*
> *1 medium onion, peeled and chopped*
> *1 clove garlic, slivered*
> *1/2 tsp. Tabasco sauce, or minced hot pepper*
> *Dash of nutmeg*
> *Salt and pepper to taste*

Blend for a few seconds and pour the sauce over the mashed fish mixture. Combine these ingredients well and add:

> *1 egg, beaten*

Mixture should be stiff enough to mold into balls about one and a half inches in diameter. If it is too dry, add the fish stock a tablespoon at a time. Fry the balls in hot, deep fat until golden brown.

Fishing boats moored in Curaçao's Schottegat Bay

Krokèchi   (Fish Croquettes)   *Serves 4*

Dissolve in one-fourth cup milk:

> *1 or 2 Tbs. gelatine*

In a saucepan blend:

> *3 Tbs. flour*
> *2 Tbs. butter*
> *$\frac{1}{4}$ cup milk*
> *$\frac{1}{2}$ cup rich chicken stock*

When the sauce is thick add:

> *1 egg yolk, beaten*
> *Dash of cream*

Continue cooking these ingredients for a few minutes but do not boil them. Remove from heat and add:

> *The dissolved gelatine*
> *Juice of one lemon*
> *2 Tbs. Chopped parsley*
> *Salt and pepper to taste*

Chop finely and add to the white sauce mixture:

> *1 cup boiled shrimp*
> *or 1 cup roasted veal*

Spread the mixture in a shallow pan and refrigerate. When firm, cut into eighths and form into cylinders. Roll the cylinders in:

> *2 or 3 lightly beaten egg whites.*

Then roll them in:

> *Bread crumbs*

Fry in deep fat until golden. Serve with parsley sprigs that have also been deepfried.

27

Entrees

Keshi Yená   (Filled Cheese Shell)   *Serves 10 - 12*

Frugality was the keynote of island living in earlier times, when provisions had to last from the visit of one sailing ship to the call of another. In this classic recipe the shell of a scooped out Edam (the thin rind remaining after a family had consumed the four pounds of cheese) is filled with spiced meat, then baked in the oven or steamed in the top of a double boiler. For these methods of preparation the red wax must be removed from the empty shell after is has been soaked in hot water. In a more dramatic version the filled Edam, with the red wax intact, is tied in cheese cloth and suspended in boiling water for twenty minutes. The wax melts away in the hot water, leaving a delicate pink blush on the cheese. Use chicken or beef for the filling.

For the chicken filling, rub with the juice of several limes:

> *1 lb. chicken breasts*
> *1 lb. chicken thighs*

Season the breasts and thighs with:

> *Salt and pepper*
> *Poultry seasoning*
> *Minced onion*

Let them stand for several hours. Then either arrange the pieces in a shallow baking dish, and after browing the chicken under the broiler, bake it for one hour at 350°, deboning it when cool enough to handle, or choose this more frugal method of preparation. Brown the chicken in three tablespoons butter, then place it in a heavy kettle with:

> *2 quarts water*
> *2 tsp. salt*
> *12 peppercorns*
> *1 or 2 onions*
> *1 celery stalk with leaves*
> *1 bay leaf, bruised*

Bring to a boil, reduce heat and simmer for twenty minutes, or just until chicken is tender. Strain and reserve the broth, discarding the vegetables. Debone the chicken and set aside. The broth is not needed for *keshi yená* and may be used for *sòpi di yuwana*, page 15.

28

Keshi Yená (cont'd)

After the chicken has been prepared by one of the above methods, sauté in two tablespoons butter:

> 3 tomatoes, peeled and chopped
> 2 onions, sliced
> 1 large green pepper, chopped
> 1 Tbs. parsley, minced, or a few drops Tabasco sauce
>   Salt and pepper

Add and stir in well:

> 2 Tbs. ketchup
> 1/4 cup pimento olives, sliced
> 1 Tbs. capers
> 1/4 cup raisins
> 2 Tbs. piccalilly
>   The chicken, or 1 lb. ground beef, lightly browned,
>   if beef is to be substituted for the chicken.

Simmer until the tomatoes are reduced, about twenty or thirty minutes. Remove from the fire and permit mixture to cool. If keshi yená is to be baked, preheat oven to 350°, if it is to be steamed, begin heating water in the bottom of a double boiler.

Beat and add to the meat mixture:

> 3 eggs, reserving about 6 Tbs.

Generously butter a casserole or the top of a double boiler. Before placing the cheese shell in it, spoon three tablespoons of the reserved beaten egg into the bottom of the container. Half fill with the meat mixture and add:

> 1 or 2 hard-cooked eggs

Fill shell to the top with remaining meat and cover with:

> The original cap of the Edam, from which
> the wax has been removed, or a few slices
> of cheese. A word of caution! Never use
> soft, young cheese for keshi yená.

Drip the remaining three tablespoonfuls of beaten egg over the top of the cheese as a sealer. (Place the lid on the double boiler). Set the casserole in a pan of hot water, or the double boiler top over the simmering water. Cook for one and one-quarter hours. Reverse keshi yená on a heated platter and keep warm for the cheese becomes hard and unappetizing if permitted to cool.

In place of the cheese shell, two pounds of Edam or Gouda slices may be used to line the cooking container. The slices should overlap and create the same effect as the shell. Add filling, cover with additional slices and follow directions for baking or steaming the shell. The traditionalist with a great deal of time and patience, may scoop out a four pound Edam or Gouda, taking care not to pierce the shell. The resulting mound of cheese may be used for bolita di keshi, page 5.

Roast Lamb "Passaat"

Serves 30

This excellent barbecue is a specialty at Zuurzak, one of Curaçao's gracious old country estates. The *passaat,* as the trade winds are locally called, plays a vital role in the preparation.

Ask the butcher to split the undersides of two young lambs, leaving the backs intact. Discard the organs, wash and dry the meat. Just before roasting, espalier the lambs on two double-T frames, as illustrated.

Build a large fire well to windward of where the guests will be. When the flame dies, pound the meat-filled frames into the earth, two and one-half or three feet to windward of the coals. The constant *passaat* permeates the meat with the flavor of the charcoal. Baste the lambs frequently with barbecue sauce. Roasting time is four hours and the coals should be kept very hot.

For the barbecue sauce, mince:

> *12 hot peppers*
> *2 large onions*

Place them in a quart jar with:

> *1 cup oil*

In a saucepan, bring to a boil:

> *1 cup tomato juice*
> *1 cup white wine vinegar*
> *2 cloves garlic, minced*
> *4 cloves*
> *1 to 2 tsp. salt*

Pour the hot liquid over the chopped peppers and onions. Fill the jar with water, cover and set aside. To bring out the full flavor of the peppers, the sauce should be made at least four days in advance.

If young kid, or *cabrito,* is barbecued instead of lamb, it may be marinated for twenty-four hours in a sauce made from equal portions of olive oil and gin, with a liberal sprinkling of herbs such as thyme, rosemary, savory, basil, etc.

30

Kapucijners   (Brown Beans in Mustard Sauce)   *Serves 6*

Kapucijners, or marrow meats, are a brown legume with a flavor all their own. Brown beans may be substituted, however, without losing the zest of the dish. Seven condiments and plain white rice accompany the *kapucijners* in this recipe.

Soak for twenty-four hours in ample water:

> *1 lb. kapucijners or brown beans*

Drain, discarding the water. Place beans in a heavy kettle with:

> *6 cups water*
> *2 tsp. salt*
> *1 large onion, studded with 3 cloves*
> *1 leek*
> *2 cloves garlic*
> *1 stalk celery with leaves*
>   *Several parsley sprigs*

Bring to a brisk boil, reduce heat and simmer for about two hours or until beans are tender. Remove vegetables from the kettle and discard. Keep the beans warm over a low flame.
In a very hot skillet melt:

> *$\frac{1}{4}$ cup butter*

Add and sear quickly:

> *1 lb. cubed sirloin steak*

Remove meat and set aside. Permit the skillet to cool, then stir into the drippings:

> *3 Tbs. flour*

Heat the skilled gently and blend in:

> *1 cup beef broth*

Stir in:

> *1 cup piccalilly*

Add beef and remove from fire. Heat this mixture gently just before serving.
Fry until crisp:

> *$\frac{1}{2}$ lb. sliced bacon*

Remove from the pan and discard drippings, reserving three table-spoonfuls. In the bacon drippings, sauté until golden but not brown:

> *4 medium onions, sliced*

Place the *kapucijners* in a serving bowl and plain white rice in another.
Arrange in seven condiment dishes surrounding the rice and beans:

> *1 or 2 raw onions, finely chopped*
> *1 cup cocktail onions, drained*   *The bacon slices*
> *1 cup dill pickles, sliced*   *The sautéed onions*
> *1 cup piccalilly*   *The sirloin in piccalilly sauce*

Island Curry

Place in a heavy kettle:

1 large chicken, about 5 pound   3 sprigs parsley
2 celery stalks   2 tsp. salt
1 or 2 onions, studded with several cloves
4 cups water

Simmer these ingredients for one-half hour or more until the chicken is tender. Strain the stock and return it to the kettle. When the chicken is cool enough to handle remove the meat in large chunks. Set the chicken aside for later use. Return the chicken bones and skin to the stock. Add one cup of water and simmer the stock for an additional forty-five minutes. Strain the stock a second time and set it aside. There should be at least four cups. Up to this point, the preparation may be made a day in advance.

When it is time to make the curry, use a large, heavy kettle to sauté:

5 Tbs. butter
4 onions coarsely chopped
1 large apple, peeled and chopped

Stir the onions and apple frequently until they are transluscent, but not browned. Remove them from the pan, pressing out the butter as it is needed for the sauce base.
Blend in:

4 Tbs. flour

Continue stirring until the flour and butter are slightly browned. Remove the kettle from the fire and permit it to cool slightly. Add the chicken broth, then return the kettle to the fire. Stir the sauce constantly until it is smooth and thick. **Add:**

1 cup raisins
Juice of $\frac{1}{2}$ lemon
Strip of lime peel

Simmer the sauce an additional five minutes then add:

1 cup light cream

The sauce now becomes an individual thing! Begin with:

2 or more tsp. curry powder (preferably Cross and
    Blackwell) mixed with a little water

With a wire whisk, stir the curry powder into the sauce. Now taste, and add more seasoning until the sauce is spicy with curry. The Antilleans may use as many as five tablespoonfuls!

Remove the strip of lime peel, and add the chicken pieces, the sautéed onions, and apple to the sauce. Warm the sauce only until the chicken is heated through, but do not boil it. Serve the curry over Coconut Rice, page 43, with any combination of the following condiments:

Chopped hard boiled eggs - Peanuts - Grated fresh ginger
Freshly grated coconut - Diced papaya - Diced bananas
Minced green pepper - Chopped green onions - Chutney
Chopped cucumber, tomatoes, and avocado - Potato sticks

Sancocho   (Rich Chicken Soup)   *Serves 6*

E ta nobo forza, the Antilleans say of *sancocho* . . . it gives you strength! A hearty, delicious chicken dish usually served at midday on Saturdays.

Rub with three tablespoons lime or lemon juice:

> *2¹/₂ lbs. chicken legs*

Make a marinada of:

> *1 medium onion, minced*
> *1 small green pepper, chopped*
> *2 stalks celery, chopped with leaves*
> *3 shallots minced*
> *2 medium tomatoes, peeled and chopped*
> *¹/₂ tsp. poultry seasoning*
> *¹/₄ tsp.nNutmeg*
> *1 tsp. cumin*
> *¹/₂ tsp. Italian seasoning*
> *Salt and pepper*

Mix with the chicken and refrigerate for twenty-four hours. Scrape the marinade from the chicken legs. Simmer it in a large kettle for ten minutes. Add the chicken legs and water to cover. Bring to a boil, reduce heat and simmer until chicken is tender, about forty minutes. Skim the surface of the broth as foam appears. Remove the chicken and strain the broth, discarding the vegetables.

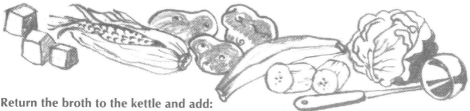

Return the broth to the kettle and add:

> *2 carrots, in thick diagonal slices*
> *¹/₂ fresh pumpkin, peeled and cut in serving pieces*

Ten minutes later, add:

> *2 firm green plantains, sliced in thick rounds*
> *(2 okumo, or white yams, quartered)*

Twenty minutes later, add:

> *3 potatoes, peeled and quartered*

For the last five minutes cooking time, add:

> *¹/₂ small cabbage, shredded*
> *2 corn-on-the-cob, broken in half.*

Return the chicken to the kettle and heat thoroughly. Serve *sancocho* in a large tureen. The vegetables may be removed from the broth at the last minute and served in a separate bowl.

33

Stobá di Carcó   (Conch Stew)   *Served 6*

Clean, peel, and pound well with a wooden mallet:
> *2 lbs. Conch meat*

Then rub it with:
> *$^1/_2$ cup white wine vinegar*

Cut the conch into bite size pieces. Sauté in three tablespoons butter:
> *1 large onion, finely chopped*
> *1 medium green pepper, finely chopped*

Add:
> *2 large tomatoes, peeled and chopped*
> *2 chicken bouillon cubes dissolved in $^1/_2$ cup water*
>   *Dash of Tabasco sauce or minced hot pepper*
> *1 Tbs. Maggi or beef extract*

Simmer the stew about twenty minutes. Add conch, cover and continue to cook only until meat is tender, about ten minutes. Adjust seasonings.

Note: As conch is now an endangered species, this recipe is included only to illustrate earlier Antillean cuisine.

Rabbit with Coconut   *Serves 6*

A speciality of Curaçao's Landhuis Klein Sint Joris where the fortunate cook has a large plantation and a family of hunters to produce the rabbit. Double the Coconut Milk recipe, page 43. Set aside.

Rub with vinegar:
> *1 plumb rabbit cut into serving pieces*

Marinate it for several hours with:
> *2 onions, chopped*
> *2 tomatoes, chopped*
> *2 or 3 celery stalks, diced*
> *1 green pepper, minced*
> *1 clove garlic, minced*
> *1 tsp. oregano leaves*
> *2 Tbs. Worcestershire sauce*
>   *Salt and pepper*

Bring the coconut milk to a boil in a heavy cast iron kettle, then add the rabbit and the marinade. Reduce the flame, and simmer the ingredients for about one-half hour. Leave the kettle uncovered and stir the meat frequently. Add:
> *3 potatoes, diced*   *A few drops of ruku, page 14*

Cover the kettle and continue cooking the stew until potatoes are tender about one-half hour. Stir the ingredients frequently, then add:
> *8 pimento olives*   *2 tsp. Capers*

Adjust seasonings, and serve the stew with *funchi*.

Dobed Turtle

Serves 4

Crossing the border from French St. Martin the term *"en daube"*, referring to meat braised in wine, becomes "dobed". This delicious recipe for sea turtle is a credit to either expression.

Rub with two or three tablespoons lime juice:

> *4 sea turtle steaks (about two pounds)*

Marinate them in the following ingredients for several hours or preferably overnight:

> *1 1/2 ounces cognac or dry sherry, or 1 cup dry white wine*
> *1 medium onion, minced*
> *1 small green pepper, chopped*
> *2 tomatoes, peeled and chopped*
> *2 sprigs parsley, minced*
> *4 or 5 cloves*
> *6 peppercorns*
> *2 sprigs fresh thyme, minced*
> *1 tsp. salt*

Note: As sea turtle is now an endangered species, this recipe is included only to illustrate earlier Antillean cuisine.

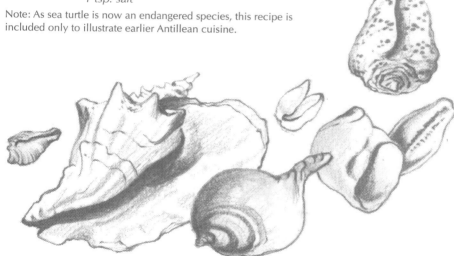

In a heavy skillet heat:

> *3 Tbs. oil*

Scrape the marinade from the steaks and brown them lightly in the oil. Add about one and one-half cups water to the meat and simmer the steaks for about twenty minutes. Add the marinade and simmer an additional half-hour, or until the turtle is tender. Adjust seasoning, and serve with fried plantains and *funchi,* which is known in the Windward Islands as Corn Meal.

Chicken Lokri

Serves 6

When Sint Maartians gather for festive occasions, this piquant combination of chicken and rice is frequently the piece de resistance of the menu.

Rub with two or three tablespoons lime juice:

> *1 three pound chicken, cut into serving pieces*

Brown it lightly in a mixture of:

> *1 Tbs. sugar*
> *2 Tbs. butter*
> *1 Tbs. tomato paste*

Add to the chicken:

> *2 celery stalks, diced*
> *2 tomatoes, peeled and chopped*
> *2 cloves garlic, minced*
> *A sprig of thyme*
> *2 tbs. Worcestershire sauce*
> *1 onion, chopped*
> *$^1/_2$ tsp. salt*

Simmer ingredients gently over a low flame until chicken is tender. Add a few tablespoonsful of water if necessary to prevent sticking.
Place in a heavy kettle:

> *$3^3/_4$ cups water*
> *$^1/_2$ tsp. salt*
> *2 chicken bouillon cubes*

Bring the water to a boil and add:

> *$1^1/_2$ cups rice*

Reduce flame and simmer for twenty minutes or until rice is fluffy and water has been absorbed.
While rice and chicken are simmering, gently braise in two tablespoons butter:

> *$^1/_2$ small cabbage, shredded*

When rice, cabbage and chicken are cooked, toss them lightly together with:

> *2 Tbs. piccalilly*
> *Dash of Tabasco sauce*

Serve the dish piping hot with fried plantains.

Pigeon Pea Soup & Dumplings

Serves 6

A favorite herb of Windward Island cooks, fresh thyme seasons this thick soup which is served as an entree. Black-eyed peas may be substituted when pigeon peas are unavailable. If one pound of fresh peas is used, the meat and stock should simmer for about forty-five minutes before the peas are added.

Soak overnight in ample water:

> $1\frac{1}{2}$ cups dried pigeon peas
> $\frac{1}{2}$ lb: salted beef or 2 salted pigs' tails

Drain both meat and peas well, and place them in a heavy kettle with:

> 4 cups fresh water
> 1 clove garlic, slivered
> 1 small onion, diced
> A sprig of thyme
> 2 Tbs. butter
> Salt and pepper to taste

Simmer until peas are tender, about one hour for dried peas, fifteen minutes for fresh ones.
Add and simmer for an additional half hour:

> 2 or 3 sweet potatoes, peeled and diced
> 1 small piece of pumpkin, peeled and diced
> 1 tsp. sugar

Simmer until the soup is slightly thick.
For the dumplings combine:

> $\frac{1}{4}$ cup flour
> 1 Tbs. corn meal
> Generous pinch of baking powder
> Pinch of salt

Add milk only until the dough is dry and stiff. To make the dumplings, pinch off bits of the dough and roll it into little balls between the palms of the hands. Drop dumplings into simmering soup about ten minutes before serving time.

Stoba di Cabrito   (Stewed Kid)   *Serves 6*

Soak overnight in ample water:

$^1/_2$ *lbs. salted beef*

Drain, discarding water. Place the beef in a heavy kettle with four cups fresh water. Bring to boil, reduce heat and simmer for about an hour. When beef is tender remove kettle from the fire. Remove the beef from the broth. Cube beef and add it once again to the kettle. Set aside for later use. Rub with three tablespoons lemon or lime juice:

1$^1/_2$ lbs. young kid, or cabrito

In a second kettle, saute in four tablespoons butter until the onion is transparent:

2 onions, sliced
2 cloves garlic, minced
1 green pepper, finely chopped
$^1/_2$ minced hot pepper or 1 tsp. Tabasco sauce

Add:

2 tomatoes, peeled and quartered
1 tsp. sugar
$^1/_4$ tsp. nutmeg
2 Tbs. ruku (See sòpi di pampuna, page 14)
The kid
Salt and pepper to taste

Simmer for thirty minutes, then pour in the beef broth and the cubed beef. Add:

3 potatoes, peeled and diced

Simmer an additional half hour, or serve when potatoes are tender. Antillean cooks add a spiny, light green cucumber, called *concomber,* to the stew at the same time as the potatoes. The cucumbers should be rasped and cut in half lengthwise. Press each half gently to pop out the seeds before adding cucumbers to the stew. If they are omitted, serve the stobá with *papaya berde,* page 47.

Saté   (Marinated Meat on Skewers)   *Serves 6 - 8*

To make the marinade for the saté, put in the container of an electric blender:

1 large onion, coarsley chopped
2 cloves garlic   *1 tsp. salt*
Juice of two lemons   *1 tsp. ground coriander for beef*
2 Tbs. sugar   *or 1 tsp. ground ginger for pork*
1 cup soy sauce   *1 cup oil*

Blend thoroughly and pour over:

5 lbs. beef or pork tenderloin, cubed

Do not marinate overnight, but only for a few hours. Place the meat on:

36 skewers

Blend well:

1 cup oil
2 Tbs. Soy sauce

Pour into a large shallow dish. To keep meat from becoming dry, roll each skewer in seasoned oil before frying. Saté is also excellent when barbecued.

Peanut Sauce

Heat three cups oil in heavy skillet, then fry until crisp:

2 large onions, thinly sliced

Drain the onions well on absorbent paper.
Place in the container of an electric blender:

1 cup water   *3 Tbs. soy sauce*
1 cup peanuts   *2 Tbs. brown sugar*
The fried onions   *Juice of two limes or an equivalent*
1 or 2 cloves garlic   *amount of tamarind juice, about 2 Tbs.*

Blend thoroughly. The sauce will always be slightly textured and rather thick. Pour it into a saucepan and bring to a boil over low heat. If it seems too thick, add water, a few tablespoonsfuls at a time, stirring well after each addition. If oil appears on the surface, stir in a few tablespoonsfuls of milk.
Remove sauce from the fire and add immediately:

1 raw onion, finely minced
1 tsp. Tabasco sauce

Indonesian cooks add *trassi*, a shrimp paste to their peanut sauce. Anchovy paste may be substituted, but only as much as adheres to the tip of a knife. A little bit goes a long way!

Complements

Banana na Binja   (Plantains in Port Wine)   *Serves 4*

Peel and cut in half lenghtwise:

>*2 very ripe plantains*

In a heavy skillet melt:

>*2 or 3 Tbs. butter*

Gently sauté the plantain halves until golden on one side. Turn them over. In a mixing bowl blend well:

>*2 or 3 Tbs. dark brown sugar*
>*2 Tbs. water*
>*2 or 3 Tbs. port wine*
>*Dash of cinnamon*

Pour mixture over the plantain halves. Simmer gently until the liquid becomes a thick syrup. Serve at once.

Banana Hasá   (Fried Plantain)   *Serves 6 - 8*

When asked to comment on Antillean cuisine, one cook remarked, "But we eat the same thing every day!" She could have been referring to the plantain, or *banana,* dishes which accompany almost every meal.

Peel and cut into thin, lengthwise slices:

>*3 very ripe plantains*

Fry until golden brown in:

>*3 or 4 Tbs. butter*

Add:

>*Pinch of salt*

Keep plantain slices warm in the oven until serving time.

Bolo di Banana   (Plantain Pudding)   *Serves 12*

Peel and cut in half lengthwise
> *5 very ripe plantains*

Melt in a heavy skillet
> *$1/3$ cup butter*

Fry the plantains until golden brown and remove from the skillet.
Stir into the drippings until sugar is dissolved:
> *$2^1/2$ cups brown sugar*
> *2 Tbs. water*

Remove from the heat. Mash the plantains well, adding the brown sugar mixture.
Grate and add to the plantains:
> *$1/2$ lb. sharp yellow cheese*

Preheat oven to 350°.
Stir in:
> *$1/2$ cup cracker crumbs*
> *2 tsp. cinnamon*
> *$1^1/2$ tsp. allspice*
> *$1/2$ cup raisins*
> *$1/2$ cup dry sherry*

Mix the ingredients well and pour into a well-buttered casserole. Bake about forty minutes. Do not permit the pudding to become dry.

Bolo di Mainshi   (Corn Pudding)   *Serves 4*

Preheat oven to 350°.
Combine in a saucepan:
> *1 Tbs. cornstarch*
> *1 Tbs. flour*
> *1 Tbs. sugar*
> *Salt to taste*

Stir in:
> *1 tin creamed corn*

Beat well:
> *2 eggs*

Add:
> *$1/2$ cup milk*
> *1 tsp. vanilla*

Stir eggs and milk into the corn mixture and add:
> *3 Tbs. melted butter*

Mix well and pour into a shallow casserole. Bake for about one hour.

Funchi (Corn-Meal Mush) *Serves 6*

Funchi, the Antillean staple, is a simple corn-meal preparation. It must be vigorously stirred while cooking, and to the rhythm of these rotations old-time cooks repeated. *Un pa mi, un pa bo, un pe. Funchi* was then scooped from the kettle with a little round calabash, and the "funchi ball" was placed on each individual plate — "One for me, one for you, one for him".

Mix in heavy saucepan:

> *1¼ cups cold water*
> *1½ cups corn-meal*
> *1 tsp. salt*

Stir in:

> *1½ cups boiling water*
> *1 Tbs. butter*

Bring to a brisk boil over high heat and cook for three minutes. Continue cooking an additional three minutes, stirring the *funchi* vigorously with a wooden spoon or *palu di funchi*. When the mixture is very stiff and pulls away from the sides of the pan, remove from the fire. Turn out into a deep, well-buttered bowl and cover with a plate. Now shake the *funchi* down in the bowl, then invert it on a serving platter.

For a special Sunday breakfast fry sliced *funchi* in butter and serve with crisp bacon and scrambled eggs.

Palu di funchi
Curaçao Museum

Coconut Milk *3 Cups*

This easy concoction greatly enhances any number of dishes. Fresh coconut gives the milk a more delicate flavor, but the desiccated meat may also be used.

Place in a saucepan:

> *1 cup grated coconut*

Pour over it:

> *3 cups boiling water*

Cover tightly and infuse (like tea) for thirty minutes. Pour liquid through a fine sieve, pressing all the moisture from the coconut. Discard the coconut, as it is now tasteless.

Tutu   (Corn-Meal Mush with Black-Eyed Peas)   *Serves 6 - 8*

Tutu is *funchi* with frills, a heartier version of the standard corn-meal dish.

Soak overnight:

>*1 cup black-eyed peas*

Drain, and bring to a boil in a heavy saucepan containing:

>*4 cups water*
>*(or 2 cups water, 2 cups coconut milk, page 43)*

Add:

>*1 cup dark brown sugar, loosely packed*
>*2 cloves garlic, crushed*
>*8 strips bacon, diced, or 1/4 lb. salted beef*
>*1½ tsp. salt*

Add four tablespoons butter if the coconut milk is omitted; omit the salt if salted beef is substituted for the bacon. Boil rapidly until peas are tender, about thirty minutes.
Gradually stir in:

>*1 cup corn-meal*

Reduce heat. Follow directions for stirring and serving *funchi*.

Hand-caved serving utensils
Curaçao Museum

Coconut Rice   *Serves 4*

Bring to a boil:

>*3 cups coconut milk*

Add:

>*1 cup rice*
>*Salt to taste*
>*1 blade lemon, or citronella grass, slightly crushed*

Bring to a second boil, reduce heat and simmer for twenty minutes or until rice is dry. Discard the citronella grass before serving. Coconut rice is an excellent accompaniment for curries.

Nasi Goreng   (Fried Rice)   *Serves 30*

A traditional rice dish from Indonesia, *nasi goreng* appears on many local menus. It is served frequently at Zuurzak as an accompaniment to Roast Lamb Passaat, page 30, and the proportions given here adequately serve thirty guests. The rice is not fried in this recipe, making such a large quantity easier to handle.

Bake in 325° oven for 1$^1/_2$ hours or until golden brown:

> *5 lb. chicken breasts*

seasoned with salt, pepper, paprika, oregano and a little oil. When chicken is cool enough to handle, debone, breaking the breast meat into chunks. Set them aside for later use.
For:

> *6 cups rice*

Prepare three saucepans, each containing:

> *5 cups boiling water*
> *2 chicken bouillon cubes*
> *$^1/_2$ tsp. salt*

Add two cups rice to each pan. Bring to a second boil, reduce heat and simmer twenty minutes or until rice is dry.

In a large skillet sauté:

> *$^1/_2$ cup butter*
> *1 Tbs. sambal oelek or Tabasco sauce*
> *$^1/_2$ pound very lean bacon*
> *5 large onions, sliced*

The onions should be transparent and golden.

Stir in:

> *4 cups chopped vegetables, such as celery, scallions,*
> *leeks, parsley, carrots*

These should be lightly sautéed, but remain crisp.
Add:

> *$^1/_4$ cup soy sauce, or to taste*

In a very large container, lightly toss together the rice, vegetable mixture and the chicken. Heap nasi goreng on large platters, which may be kept warm in the oven until serving time.

Pigeon Peas & Rice

Serves 6

Like *funchi* in the south, this hearty dish accompanies almost any meal in the Windward Islands. Black-eyed peas may be substituted when pigeon peas are not available.

Soak overnight in ample water:

> *1 cup dried pigeon peas*

Drain them well and place peas in a heavy kettle with:

> *4 cups fresh water*
> *1 or 2 cloves garlic, minced*
> *1 medium onion, minced*
> *A sprig of fresh thyme*
> *2 Tbs. butter*
> *Salt and pepper*

Bring these ingredients to a boil, reduce heat, and simmer them for about one-half hour. Add:

> *1 cup rice*

(If fresh peas are used, add one-half pound of them to the kettle with the rice). There should be about two and one-half cups liquid with the peas and rice. Simmer the combined ingredients for about twenty minutes, stirring occasionally until rice is fluffy and the water is absorbed. This dish may be served either hot or cold.

Onion Custard

Serves 6

The Pasanggrahan Guest House, Sint Maarten's renowned hostelery where Queen Juliana of the Netherlands once lodged, serves this delicate dish at traditional holiday meals. It replaces creamed onions, but is infinitely lighter in consistency.

Preheat oven to 325°.
Simmer in butter until transluscent:

> *6 medium onions, diced*

Combine the following ingredients:

> *2 eggs, beaten*   *1 cup milk*
> *¼ cup butter, melted*   *1 tsp. salt*
> *Nutmeg and pepper to taste*

Stir in the sautéed onions. Pour the mixture into a well-buttered casserole and bake twenty-five minutes or until custard is set.

Johnny Cakes

Serves 4 - 6

Throughout the Antilles the best cooks agree that "it takes a person from Sint Maarten to make good Johnny Cakes"! The ingredients are listed here, but the Sint Maarten touch is a bit more exclusive.

Sift before measuring:

> *2 cups flour*

Resift it with:

> *2 tsp. baking powder*
> *1 tsp. salt*

Using two knives or a pastry blender, cut into the flour:

> *2 Tbs. butter*

Combine and stir until the sugar is dissolved:

> *$^1/_3$ cup water*
> *2 tsp. sugar*

To make dough, add the liquid a little at a time to the flour. Turn the dough onto a floured surface and knead it well. Pinch off pieces, roll them into small balls and flatten into circles two inches in diameter and one-fourth inch thick. Or roll out dough to the same thickness and cut circles with a cookie cutter. Fry the cakes in hot fat until they are puffy and golden. (A cast iron skillet is ideal for this, but it must be kept heavily greased by adding oil from time to time while the cakes are frying). Drain the cakes on absorbent paper and keep them warm in the oven. Breakfast johnny cakes are delicious when split and buttered immediately. Smaller cakes, filled with cream cheese, may be served at tea time.

Soufflé di Berehena   (Eggplant Soufflé)   *Serves 6*

Preheat oven to 350°.
Sauté in two tablespoons butter until the onion is transparent:

> *1 medium onion, minced*
> *$^1/_2$ green pepper, finely chopped*

Add:

> *1 pimento, minced*
> *2 Tbs. tomato paste*
> *Salt and pepper*

Simmer for three minutes and set the mixture aside.
Peel and dice:

> *2 large or 4 small eggplants*

Simmer them in salted water until tender. Drain and mash. Set the eggplant aside for later use.
Melt in a large saucepan.

> *3 Tbs. butter*

Stir in:

> *3 Tbs. flour*

With a wire whisk, stir in rapidly:

> *3/4 cup chicken stock or milk*

Cook over low heat, stirring constantly until mixture thickens.
Blend in:

> *$^1/_2$ cup grated Parmesan or Romano cheese*

Stir in the eggplant and tomato sauce.
Beat separately the whites and yolks of:

> *4 eggs*

Add the yolks to the eggplant mixture, then gently fold in the whites. Pour into a buttered casserole and bake forty-five minutes, or until puffed and golden brown.

Papaya Berde   (Stewed Green Papaya)   *Serves 4*

Select:

> *1 very green, medium papaya*

Peel and slice. There should be about two cups of fruit. Drop it into rapidly boiling salted water. Simmer for about one-half hour, or until fruit is tender. Drain well.
Add:

> *1 Tbs. butter*
> *Dash of nutmeg*

This fine dish is an excellent acompaniment to the *stobas,* or stews.

Desserts

Forgotten Pudding   (Carmelized Meringue)   *Serves 10*

True to its name, this delicate meringue is placed in the oven and promptly forgotten.

Preheat the oven to 450°. Then carmelize:

> $^1/_2$ cup sugar

and pour immediately into the mold in which the meringue is to be baked.

Beat until completely dry:

> 8 egg whites
> $^1/_8$ tsp. cream of tartar

Beat in:

> 6 rounded tsp. sugar

Spoon egg whites over the carmelized sugar. Set the mold in a pan of hot water and place in the oven. TURN OFF THE OVEN IMMEDIATELY, and leave the meringue for two hours. Serve with custard sauce.

Custard Sauce

Mix together in the top of a double boiler:

> 2 or 3 Tbs. sugar
> 2 Tbs. flour
>   Pinch of salt

Stir in:

> 3 beaten egg yolks

Add:

> $1^1/_2$ cups scalded milk

Cook over hot water, stirring constantly, until mixture thickens. Cool, stirring occasionally. If necessary, strain the sauce. Add:

> 1 tsp. vanilla

To serve, spoon the sauce over the meringue.

Kesío   (Caramel Custard)   *Serves 4*

In the top of a double boiler, but directly over a low flame, place:

> *3 Tbs. sugar*

Melt slowly, stirring constantly with a wooden spoon, until the sugar becomes a caramel syrup. Remove from fire and cool.
Slightly beat:

> *4 eggs*
> *Pinch of salt*

Add gradually:

> *4 Tbs. sugar*

Beat well until the sugar is dissolved.
Slowly stir in:

> *1½ cups hot milk*
> *1 tsp. vanilla*

Strain the mixture into the double boiler containing the caramelized sugar. Place over gently simmering water for about forty minutes, or until a silver knife inserted in the center comes out free of custard. Remove from the fire, and cool immediately in the double boiler.
At serving time unmold the kesio on to a shallow platter. If some of the caramel clings to the pan, heat gently until it melts. Cool slightly and pour over the unmolded kesio.

Soenchi   (Meringue Kisses)   *8 Confections*

Local recipes are frequently well-guarded secrets! The authors were refused a *soenchi* recipe by an Aruban friend, who explained that her mother banished everyone from the kitchen when she whipped up her celebrated meringues. Be content with this substitute, for a *soenchi* can always be traded for the real thing.

Preheat oven to 250°.
Beat until stiff and dry:

> *1 egg white*

Gradually stir in:

> *1½ Tbs. sugar*
> *A drop of red or green food coloring*

Soenchi should be lightly tinted, never boldly colored.
Drop by teaspoonfuls on a lightly greased cookie sheet.
Place in the oven for about one hour. Permit to cool and serve at once. If neglected, soenchis absorb moisture and become sticky.

Windward Island Pies

2 Servings

The crust for traditional Windward Island pies is a rich, cake-like pastry which is easy to handle. It is patted into place in the pie pan, and does not require rolling out. The following recipe is sufficient for one deep 10" crust, plus the decorative pastry swirls illustrated below.

Preheat the oven to 350°.

Combine in a large mixing bowl:

> $^3/_4$ *cup butter*
> $^3/_4$ *cup sugar*

Beat well and add:

> *1 egg*
> *3 Tbs. cold water*

Sift before measuring:

> *4 cups flour*

Resift it with:

> *1 tsp. baking powder*
> $^1/_2$ *tsp. salt*

Stir the sifted ingredients into the butter and egg mixture, then knead the dough on a lightly floured surface. It should remain soft and spongy. If the dough seems heavy, sprinkle it lightly with water and knead it a second time. Pat the pastry into place, leaving a generous over-hang of dough around the rim of the pie pan. This is later folded over the filling to make a wide band of top crust around the edge of the pie. Place one of the following fillings — page 51 — in the pastry shell, and brush the top crust and decorations with:

> *1 egg, well beaten*

Cover the pie tightly with aluminium foil and place it in the preheated oven. Remove the foil fifteen minutes later, but continue baking the pie an additional half-hour, or until the crust is golden.

For the pastry swirls, roll a strip of dough about five inches long. Coil it, then flatten it with the palm of the hand. Place the coils close together to form an open crust.

50

Windward Island Pies (cont'd)

Banana Filling

In a mixing bowl place:

5 or 6 large, ripe bananas, or bacobas,
peeled and sliced into rounds (See Banana Chips)

Sprinkle them with:

Juice of 1 or 2 limes

Combine:

$^1/_4$ cup sugar
1 tsp. cinnamon

Dust the banana rounds with this mixture, tossing the slices lightly so they are evenly coated. Fill the prepared pie shell and arrange the top crust and pastry decorations.

Baking instructions are the same for both fillings.

Cashew Filling

This elegant filling calls for cashew fruit instead of the familiar nut, which grows outside its red, cloche-like fruit. Select at least.

12 ripe cashews

Discard the nuts and prick the skin of each cashew fruit several times with a fork. Squeeze out the juice which, though rich in Vitamin C, is extremely tart and bitter. Place the fruit in an enamel or pyrex sauce pan with:

2 cinnamon sticks

Combine and pour over the fruit:

5 cups sugar
4 cups water

Bring these ingredients to a boil. Reduce the heat, and simmer the cashews for about an hour, stirring gently from time to time to prevent sticking. The fruit should remain in tact. When the liquid has become a thick syrup, drain the fruit well. Place it in the pie shell and bake as directed. The cashew syrup may replace the lime sauce served with *Pudin di Coco*, page 53.

Dushi di Tamarijn   (Candied Tamarind)   *3 Cups*

Dushi di tamarijn is a bonus reaped from the syrup recipe, page 60.

Discard any seeds or shell clinging to the drained fruit. Place the soaked tamarinds in a large saucepan and add:

> *3 cups water*

Place over high heat and boil vigorously for ten minutes.
Remove from the fire and stir in:

> *5 cups sugar*
> *10 allspice*

Return to the heat and boil vigorously for twenty or thirty minutes, removing any froth which appears on te surface. The liquid should boil down to a thick syrup. Discard the allspice, and when the fruit is cool spoon it into a serving bowl. With the fingers lift each *dushi* from the preserve by the bit of stem, which makes a small handle.

Bolo di Rom   (Rum Cake)   *15 Serving*

When made with *laraha,* the bitter Curaçao orange, this cake exudes a pungent aroma even when cooled. Grated lemon peel and lemon juice may be substituted for the orange without loss of the cake's unusual taste.

Preheat oven to 350°. Then cream:

> *1 cup butter   1$\frac{1}{2}$ cups sugar*

Add one at a time, beating after each addition:

> *6 eggs*

Blend in:

> *$\frac{3}{4}$ cup laraha, or bitter orange, juice*
> *$\frac{1}{4}$ cup grated laraha, or bitter orange, peel*

Sift and add to the batter:

> *1$\frac{1}{2}$ cups all purpose flour*
> *1 cup yellow corn meal*
> *2 tsp. baking powder*

Stir in:

> *$\frac{1}{4}$ cup rum*

Pour batter into a lightly greased 10" pyrex baking dish. It should be at least 2" deep. Bake for approximately forty minutes.
Melt over gently boiling water, then beat well to remove any lumps:

> *4 squares bittersweet chocolate*

While the cake is still warm from the oven, spread it with the melted chocolate. The icing should be permitted to harden before the cake is served.

Pudin di Coco   (Coconut Pudding)   *Serves 6*

Soak in one-fourth cup rum:

> *2 Tbs. gelatine*

In a saucepan combine:

> *3 egg yolks, beaten until creamy*
> *1/4 cup sugar*

Stir in:

> *1 cup coconut milk, page 43*
> *1 cup milk*

Cook over low heat, stirring constantly, until mixture thickens. Blend in the gelatine until it dissolves. Chill in the refrigerator until the mixture begins to thicken.

Beat until stiff but not dry:

> *3 egg whites*
> *Pinch of salt*

Gradually add while beating:

> *$1/4$ cup sugar*

In a separate bowl whip until stiff:

> *1 cup heavy cream*

Beat the custard mixture with a wire whisk, then fold it gently into the egg whites. Fold in the whipped cream. Mound the pudding in a serving bowl and chill until firm. Serve with lime sauce. See below.

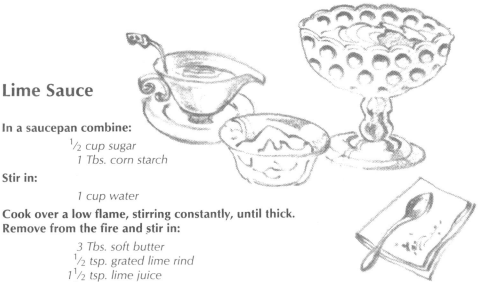

Lime Sauce

In a saucepan combine:

> *$1/2$ cup sugar*
> *1 Tbs. corn starch*

Stir in:

> *1 cup water*

Cook over a low flame, stirring constantly, until thick.
Remove from the fire and stir in:

> *3 Tbs. soft butter*
> *$1/2$ tsp. grated lime rind*
> *$1 1/2$ tsp. lime juice*
> *$1/8$ tsp. salt*

Chill well. Just before serving beat sauce with a wire whisk.

Bolo Pretu   (Dark Fruit Cake)   *2 Five-Pound Cakes*

Bolo pretu, or black cake, thickly iced and aglitter with tiny silver balls, is the Antillean wedding cake. Keepsake slices, placed in small white boxes inscribed in silver with the initials of the bridal couple, are distributed to guests at the wedding reception. Without the trimmings *bolo pretu* is a popular every-day dessert which keeps for six months or more if refrigerated.

Chop as finely as possible in a food grinder:

2 lbs. raisins	*1 lb. glazed lime peel*
2 lbs. prunes	*(1 lb. glazed papaya*
2 lbs. currants	*may be substituted*
1 lb. glazed lemon peel	*for lime peel)*

Place the fruits in a large earthenware bowl and mix well. Pour over them and blend in well:

> *2 cups dark Karo syrup*
> *1 bottle Cherry Heering*
> *(25 ounces or about $^4/_5$ quart)*
> *$^1/_4$ bottle cognac (6 ounces or $^3/_4$ cup)*

Cover and set aside for at least two days, but preferably for one week.

Chop as finely as possible in the food grinder:

> *1 lb. almonds (1$^1/_4$ lb. bitter almonds)*

Sift:

> *1 lb. flour*

Set almonds and flour aside for later use.
Preheat oven to 300°.
Cream:

> *1$^1/_2$ lbs. butter*
> *1 lb. brown sugar*
> *2 tsp. cinnamon*
> *2 tsp. nutmeg*
> *1 tsp. ground cloves*

Beat and add to the creamed mixture:

> *20 eggs*

Add the fruits and the almonds. Stir in the flour.
Grease two baking pans. They should be at least 2$^1/_4$" deep and 10" in diameter. Cover them with greased brown paper. Divide the batter equally between the two pans. Bake for one hour, then test with a toothpick at fifteen minute intervals to determine when the cakes are done. The toothpick should be free of batter when withdrawn from the center of the cakes. When thoroughly cooled, wrap cakes in aluminum foil and store in air-tight containers, preferably in the refrigerator. Sprinkle a bit of cognac over them from time to time.

Carrot Cake

Preheat oven to 325°.
Grate finely until there are 1^1/$_2$ cups:

>*5 or more large carrots (one pound)*

Sift before measuring:

>*2 cups flour*

Resift it with:

>^{1}/$_2$ *tsp. soda*
>*1 tsp. baking powder*
>*1 tsp. cinnamon*
>^{1}/$_4$ *tsp. ground ginger*
>^{1}/$_4$ *tsp. ground cloves*
>*Pinch of salt*

Set the sifted ingredients
aside for later use.
Beat:

>*3 eggs*

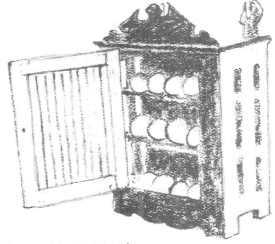

Antique egg rack.   Courtesy Mrs. W.P. Maal

Add:

>*1^1/$_2$ cups white or brown sugar, firmly packed*
>   *(Local cooks add an additional ^{1}/$_2$ cup sugar)*
>*1 cup oil*

Blend in the carrots and the sifted ingredients
For a richer cake add:

>^{1}/$_2$ *cup chopped walnuts*
>*1 cup raisins*
>*1 cup glazed mixed fruit*

Line a 10" pan with waxed paper and grease it lightly.
Bake the cake for about one hour. When it is cool place a paper doilie over
the top. Sift powdered sugar over the cake, and carefully remove the doilie.
An attractive sugar pattern remains.

Coconut Cake

Serves 12

Preheat oven to 300°.
Cream together:

> 1 cup butter   2 cups sugar

Add, one at a time, and beat well after each addition:

> 6 eggs

Sift, then measure:

> 2 cups flour

Stir the flour into the butter mixture.
Add:

> 2 cups grated coconut   1 tsp. vanilla

Lightly grease a deep 10" cake pan and dust it with flour. Spread the batter evenly in the pan, and bake the cake for one hour at 300°. Reduce heat to 200° and leave cake in the oven an additional twenty minutes. No icing is necessary as it detracts from the cake's refreshing flavor.

Sweet Potato Pie

Serves 12

A typical Windward Isle dessert, this savory pie is a speciality of the Pasanggrahan Guest House in Sint Maarten.

Follow the pastry directions for Windward Island Pies, page 50. Pat the crust into a 10" pie pan, fill and bake as a Windward Island pie.

Peel and dice into cubes:

> 4 or 5 yams

Simmer them in salted water until tender. Drain and mash the yams, removing any lumps. Add to the mashed yams and mix well:

> 4 eggs, slightly beaten
> $\frac{1}{2}$ cup white or brown sugar, firmly packed
> $\frac{1}{2}$ tsp. salt $\frac{1}{2}$ tsp. allspice
> 1 tsp. cinnamon $\frac{1}{8}$ tsp. nutmeg
> A grating of fresh ginger

Add and mix well:

> $1\frac{1}{2}$ cups light cream
> 2 Tbs. rum

Adjust seasonings and spoon the mixture into the pie shell. Bake for an hour, or until the custard is set and a knife inserted in the filling is clean when withdrawn.

Chobolobo   (Mango Flambée)   *Serves 6*

The Curaçao liqueur called for in this mango flambee is the geniune Senior C.O.C., Curaçao of Curaçao, made from a bitter orange called *laraha* which grows on the island.

Depending upon their size, choose:

> *4 or 6 firm, ripe mangoes*

Slice and cover with:

> *2 or 3 Tbs. lime juice, in which*
> *a little sugar has been dissolved.*

Set aside. Purée the mangoes if they seem stringy. In a chafing dish combine and sautée gently:

> *$1/_2$ tsp. orange or lime peel*
> *1 Tbs. brown sugar*
> *2 Tbs. butter*
> *1 jigger each banana,*
>   *maraschino and*
>   *Curaçao liqueurs*

Add the mangoes and blend with the sauce. Cradle a silver ladle on the fruit and fill it with:

> *$1/_3$ cup warmed cognac*

These preparations should be made in the kitchen. Bring the chafing dish to the table. Ignite the cognac in the ladle and pour it, flaming, over the mangoes.
Serve over:

> *Vanilla ice cream*

Cocada   (Coconut Candy)   *About 3 Cups*

In a saucepan combine:

> *1 lb. brown sugar*
> *1 cup water*

Simmer gently until mixture forms a thick syrup. Have a cup of cold water ready. Drop a little of the boiling syrup into it. When the syrup can be gathered up in the fingers as a soft ball, remove the saucepan from the fire. Stir in immediately:

> *1 lb. fresh grated coconut*
> *Juice of $1/_2$ lime*

Turn out on a lightly buttered platter and spread to cool.
Traditionally *cocada* is served on broken bits of the coconut shell.

Panlevi (Sponge Cookies)

Telephone conversations criss-cross Curaçao each morning as various family members are inquired about. One result of these calls may be a hastily concocted batch of *panlevi,* light sponge cookies, which are dispatched to a grandchild, niece or nephew, feeling out of sorts and home from school.

Preheat the oven to 325°.
Beat until frothy:

4 eggs

Gradually stir in:

1 cup sugar

Add:

¼ tsp. mace   *1 tsp. vanilla*

Sift and fold in:

2½ cups flour   *Pinch of salt*

Drop the batter by tablespoonfuls on a lightly greased cookie sheet dusted with flour. Batter should form a peaked mound. Cookies should be about two and a half inches in diameter. Bake twenty minutes, or until edges are lightly browned. The *panlevi* should be at once crisp and chewy.

Château (Chocolate Trifle)

Prepare *pan levi* as indicated above.
Melt over boiling water, or a very low flame:

4 ounces unsweetend baking chocolate

Add a little at a time:

1½ cups rich cream

Beat long and hard as there should be no lumps. Chill thoroughly.
Beat until light and creamy:

2 cups butter

Beat in:

3½ cups confectioners sugar, sifted

Beat in one at a time:

4 eggs

Add:

1 tsp. vanilla

Blend in the chilled chocolate mixture.
Place five or six *panlevi* in the bottom of a large serving bowl. Cover with a layer of the chocolate. Add a second layer of *panlevi,* pressing the cookies into the chocolate. Repeat until the bowl is full, finishing with a layer of chocolate. Garnish with snipped maraschino cherries and slivered almonds. Refrigerate overnight and serve well chilled.

Arepita di Pampuna
24 small pancakes

Little golden pancakes which replace crackers when served with a mild white cheese.

Peel, cube and cook until tender:
>   *2 lbs. fresh pumpkin*

Drain it well, then purée thoroughly. Add:
>   *2 eggs, beaten*
>   *2 scant cups milk*
>   *1 tsp. vanilla*

Sift together:
>   *1 cup flour*
>   *4 Tbs. sugar, or to taste*
>   *1 tsp. salt*
>   *1 tsp. cinnamon*

Fold the flour mixture into the pumpkin purée. If the batter is too thin, add more flour; if too thick, add little milk. Drop by tablespoonfuls on to a lightly oiled griddle. Flip pancakes once and bake until golden.

Crema di Sorsaka   (Soursap Bavarian Cream)   *Serves 6*

Select:
>   *2 medium ripe soursaps*

Peel, seed and rub pulp through a sieve. Divide into two equal portions and set aside.

Soak in one-fourth cup cold water:
>   *2 Tbs. gelatine*

In a saucepan scald:
>   *$1^3/_4$ cup milk or light cream*

Add, stirring until dissolved:
>   *$^1/_2$ cup sugar*
>   *Pinch of salt*

Blend in gelatine until it dissolves. Then stir in one portion of the soursap purée. To the second portion add sugar to taste and chill in the refrigerator for later use. Chill the gelatine mixture until it begins to thicken, then whip until fluffy with a wire whisk.

Beat until stiff:
>   *1 cup heavy cream*

Fold it into the gelatine mixture. Heap the pudding into a serving dish and chill thoroughly. Just before serving, spoon the remaining soursap over de pudding.

Beverages

Prickly Pear Punch

About 3 Quarts

Scrape the spines from:

> *1 lb. prickly pear fruit*

Place the fruit in a large kettle with:

> *3 cups sugar*   *A cinnamon stick*
> *2 cups water*

Simmer these ingredients over a low flame until they form a thick syrup, Remove the kettle from the fire and add:

> *1 tsp. vanilla*

Strain the syrup through a double thickness of cheesecloth, making sure that no prickly pear spines find their way into the syrup. When the syrup is thoroughly cool, add:

> *A fifth of rum*

A few drops of orange food coloring give the punch a brighter hue.

Stropi di Tamarijn   (Tamarind Concentrated)   *1 Quart*

Select

> *Large, plump green tamarinds*

Shell them, leaving a bit of the stem attached to each fruit. Score each tamarind deeply along the stem side, cutting throughly the pulp to the seed. Place fruit in a three-quart pyrex or enamel saucepan until the pan is three-fourths full. Cover the fruit with water and let stand for twenty-four hours, or until the seeds float to the surface of the water.

Strain and reserve the liquid, which will be very bitter. To remove all sediment and any bits of shell, strain the liquid a second time through a double thickness of cheesecloth. If necessary, add water to make five cups, and return the liquid to the saucepan.

Stir in until dissolved:

> *4 cups sugar*

Place on high heat and boil vigorously for at least twenty minutes. Skim off any foam appearing on the surface. Permit the syrup to cool. It should have a clear, amber color. If stored in a sterilized container, tamarind syrup will keep indefinitely in the refrigerator. To serve, pour syrup over ice cubes and dilute to taste with cold water. See *dushi di tamarijn,* page 52.

Ponche Crema   (Eggnog)   *About 1 Quart*

Deliciously rich and generously laced with rum, *ponche crema* is a favorite with the "Aunties" who never touch spirits. It is served with tiny spoons in the tiniest of glasses, and rarely does a drop remain. One wonderful cook used to make *ponche crema* to sell in the neighborhood *tokos,* or markets. She had two recipes, one commercial and one for home consumption. The secret of the *ponche crema* served at home is revealed here for the first time.

Grate:

> *1 tsp. fresh nutmeg*

into:

> *2 Tbs. white Bacardi rum*

Set aside.
Take:

> *3 eggs and 3 egg yolks*

Carefully remove the coagulated spots which cling to the yolks of fertilized eggs. Beat eggs and yolks with a wire whisk until light and frothy
Add:

> *1 tin condensed milk*
> *(397 grams or about 1¹⁄₂ cups)*

Using the milk tin as a measure blend in well:

> *A quantity of rum equal to that of the*
> *condensed milk*

Add:

> *1 small tin evaporated milk*
> *(170 grams or about ²⁄₃ cup)*

Beat again.
Decant the rum which has been soaking with the nutmeg into the egg and milk mixture. Be sure that the nutmeg grains do not find their way into the *ponche crema.*
Add:

> *1 generous tsp. vanilla*

Pour the mixture into the top of a double boiler. Cook over gently boiling water, stirring constantly, until the liquid thickens, about fifteen minutes. Set aside to cool.

When the *ponche crema* is thoroughly chilled, funnel it into a sterilized, untinted decorative whiskey or wine bottle. Cap well and refrigerate indefinitely. *Ponche crema,* which is called *coddle* in the Windward Isles, has a creamy consistency and resembles eggnog in flavor.

Beauperthuy Punch

Monsieur Beauperthuy was Mayor of Marigot in French St. Martin, but his fame spread to the Dutch side with this well-know punch.

As illustrated, spiral the peeling from ten limes. Scrape away any white pulp and drop the spirals into a fifth of rum. Set the bottle aside for at least a week. The longer the lime steeps in the rum, the better the punch.
For the syrup, combine in a heavy saucepan:

> 2 cups sugar
> 1 cup water

Stir these only until the sugar is dissolved. Then cook the mixture over a low flame, without stirring, until a little of the syrup forms a soft ball when dropped into a cup of cold water. When syrup has reached the soft ball stage, remove it from the fire. It should be kept in the refrigerator when not in use. The rum and syrup are combined in varying proportions to produce Beauperthuy Punch. With more syrup it becomes an after-dinner liqueur. Less syrup and a tot of the rum produce a refreshing drink for any time of day.

Mawby   4 Quarts

To create this delicious Windward Island drink, both a supply of bark and a fermented bottle of Mawby are necessary.

Place in a large kettle:

> 3 quarts water
> 1/4 lb. bark of the mawby tree
> 3 or 4 cloves
> 1 tsp. anise seed
> 1 small piece orange peel

Keep these ingredients at a brisk boil for fifteen minutes.
Remove the kettle from the flame, and add;

> 1 tsp. vanilla

Permit the liquid to stand overnight, than strain it through a double thickness of cheesecloth. Sweeten the Mawby to taste with:

> Brown sugar

Now add one quart of fermented Mawby to the new brew. Have three sterilized quart bottles ready. Fill each one, cork it tightly, and set the Mawby aside until fermentation is complete (about one-half day in the tropics). Be sure to reserve one bottle of Mawby for the next brew.

Index
and Glossary

Index
and Glossary